Yeah right. Again!

Tui

Yeah right. Again!

Hodder Moa

For all New Zealanders who got a laugh out of the billboards, especially those who managed to laugh at themselves.

Introduction

Societies throughout the ages have had their social commentators: Ancient Greece had Socrates, Germany had Marx and in New Zealand it's Tui — yeah right!

With its unique twist on life in the colonies, Tui puts kiwi trials and tribulations in the stocks, having a laugh at anything it can. From political scandals, clingy girlfriends and New Zealand TV to serious news events, metrosexuals and sleeping with your flatmate, nothing (and we mean nothing) is sacred.

It's been lots of fun stirring up the nation with the ***Yeah Right*** billboards over this past year. It took many hard nights for the smart alecs at Tui to come up with the perfect lines, and all suggestions were welcomed with open arms. We got some stunners from the Tui website, competitions in bars and most of all, from you, the Tui drinkers.

Little Johnny
Halfback, tour guide and Tui ambassador

Five billion chimneys in one night.

Yeah right.

Tui

Time to dust off the budgie smugglers.

Yeah right.

Tui

Let Tim build the stadium in Invercargill.

I came on the tour to see how the beer's made.

Yeah right.
Tui

**I don't need a map,
I never get lost.**

Yeah right.

Another day older, another day wiser.

Yeah right.

Tui

20 y/o male seeks long-term relationship.

Yeah right.

Tui

Auckland will be just like Paris without the billboards.

Yeah right.

Tui

I'm working from home today.

I'll do the dishes after the game.

Yeah right.

Tui

Civil Defence will save us.

vil Defence systems questioned following apparent tsunami threat to the Gisborne region.

I spent ages choosing it for you.

She was a stunner.

Yeah right.

Tui

My body is a temple.

CU ltr 4 a latte

$280,000,000 has really made a difference to our roads.

Yeah right.

Tui

It only happened once.

Yeah right.

Tui

Summer is more than beer, BBQs and bikinis.

Yeah right.

Tui

Lotto — it wouldn't change me.

We don't sponsor rugby to sell beer.

I love it when you talk during the rugby.

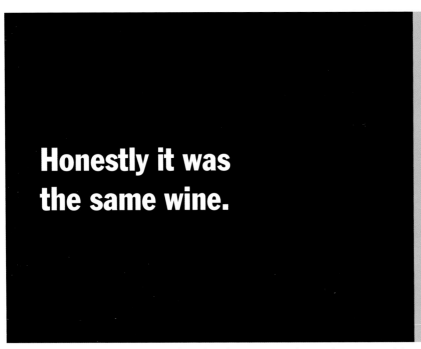

Honestly it was the same wine.

Yeah right.

Tui

Doubts raised over eligibility of a wine from a top winemaker entered into premier New Zealand wine awards.

It was like I owned the dance floor.

You'll hardly notice those pylons.

Yeah right.

Tui

Transpower's proposed powerline through the Waikato to Auckland meets resistance from landowners.

We'll keep the flat warming low key.

Yeah right.

Tui

High petrol prices in 2006.

I just want to hold you.

Yeah right.

Tui

Cool ring tone.

Yeah right.

Tui

A stadium for all New Zealanders.

It's a six-year degree.

I lost your number.

Yeah right.

Tui

It was a mutual break up.

Here honey, you have the remote.

I was going to quit anyway.

Yeah right.

Tui

NZ Idol: Ticket to Stardom

Yeah right.

Tui

It'll clear up in a couple of days.

Yeah right.

Tui

Mate, can you rub sunscreen on my back?

Wait, let's think about this first.

Yeah right.

Tui

**The Christmas ham
is still good.**

Vrrrrrrm, PISH!
Vrrrrrrm, PISH!

Yeah right.

Tui

Bikinis are sooooo overrated.

For Sale: Affordable first home in Ponsonby.

I just can't justify a six-burner barbie.

Yeah right.

Tui

51

I wear the lycra
for the ladies.

It's leaking, but the developer will pay.

Mate, I really like your pink shirt.

Tape the women's weightlifting for me.

Yeah right.

Tui

There is definitely money in that account.

Yeah right.

Tui

We apologise for
the inconvenience.

You cook dinner and I'll clean the toilet.

A threesome?
Nah, early start tomorrow.

Yeah right.

Tui

Changing the law makes it OK.

Yeah right.

Tui

Special legislation introduced to cover 2005 election over-spending.

FW: This is so funny . . .

A patrol car is on its way.

Yeah right.

Tui

I spent heaps on
your present.

I've never even seen her before.

Yeah right.

Tui

Loving mail-order bride.

Yeah right.

**Well officer here's
what happened . . .**

The bach sleeps four, max.

Yeah right.

Tui

You can't cook that on the barbie.

It won't affect local retailers.

Yeah right.

Tui

Get those cheerleaders out of my face.

Yeah right.

Tui

I'll just walk you to the door.

Yeah right.

Tui

Ask the blonde, she's in charge.

My new flatmate's giving me the eye.

Yeah right.

Tui

TAGGERS ARE COOL.

Yeah right.

Tui

The tissues are for my cold.

Yeah right.

Tui

We've got the police numbers just right.

Yeah right.

Tui

These photos are just for us.

Yeah right.

**Wouldn't have picked
Winston as a sore loser.**

Attractive 40 y/o seeks companion.

Yeah right.

Tui

I bought the boat for the family.

Yeah right.

Tui

I never doubted Mitch.

Yeah right.

Tui

I'm not a boy racer,
I'm a car enthusiast.

It will be ready on time and on budget.

Yeah right.

Tui

Mate, do you need a hug?

Politicians: role models to the nation.

Thanks. I've always wanted a crochet photo frame.

Yeah right.

Tui

There are plenty more whales in the sea.

Bring back carless days.

Yeah right.

Tui

I met this really fantastic chick on the Internet.

Yeah right.

Tui

90

It was the dog.

Yeah right.

Tui

Let's holiday with your parents.

Yeah right.

Tui

She was big boned.

This has never happened to me before.

We were going to unbundle anyway.

Telecom forced to unbundle the local loop to open up the telecommunications market.

I'm still at work.

Yeah right.

Tui

The handycam?
It's not even on.

You're right honey, I should know better.

Yeah right.

Tui

Click here for free access.

Yeah right.

Tui

I don't mind if you date my sister.

Yeah right.

Tui

I'm test-driving a hybrid.

Yeah right.

Tui

We roughed it in
Pauanui this summer.

Yeah right.

Tui

I can fix it.

Yeah right.

Tui

Don't worry, they're only staying a few nights.

It's going to be a long hot summer.

Of course I like your Mum.

Yeah right.

The road signs came with the flat.

Yeah right.

Tui

Wait, how many carbs are in this jug?

Yeah right.

Tui

Dad's new boyfriend
seems nice.

Suva for New Years?

Yeah right.

Tui

I'm going to study really hard this year.

It's only a log of wood.

Yeah right.

Tui

The credit card's only for emergencies.

Yeah right.

Tui

My Cabinet's leak proof.

Yeah right.

Tui

Dude, don't touch the hair.

I dye my hair ginger
for the ladies.

Yeah right.

It was a working lunch at Showies.

Trust me, I've done this before.

One cable should do the trick.

Yeah right.

Tui

ahuhu substation cable failure that knocked out power to most of Auckland.

I'm pretty sure I work the hardest around here.

Yeah right.

Tui

120